Praise for *Woman Life Freedom*

Woman! Life! Freedom! A chant as needed now as ever before! Writers from around the world in this throbbing volume of poetry, pen searing and soaring poems that move the human soul. This collection is a small but mighty triumph for the voices of those who believe in freedom, freedom for the women of Iran and for all women.

—**Lillian Allen**, Toronto's Poet Laureate, author of *Make the World New*

Woman Life Freedom: Poems for the Iranian Revolution features a chorus of voices that both roar and unite, mourn and revive, inviting a feminist movement onto the page. This collection captures the relentless courage of Kurdish and Iranian women, echoing their century-old struggle for justice, dignity, and liberation. The death of Jina (Mahsa) Amini sparked an uprising, manifesting as fierce resilience. In this collection, poets bear witness, lament, and demand freedom. Their words shatter apathy, haunt, and heal, in forms as diverse as the lives they honor and the beauty they unveil amid adversity and atrocities. This is poetry that rages and reckons—a passionate literary revolution.

—**Ava Homa**, author of *Daughters of Smoke and Fire*

Revolutions that aren't merely a changing of the guard take place in the mind and heart first. That is what lifts off every page in this anthology. Every poem acts as a world unto itself, providing a window into a protracted cry for freedom, best encapsulated in three simple words. Woman. Life. Freedom. It is a universal theme and that's what makes this book so important because movements of the mind are not confined by borders and boundaries. The words in this book offer an archival contribution to a spark that led to a fire and that currently smoulders within the ashes. A great archive of a moment and a movement that is on-going.

—**Samira Mohyeddin**, journalist and broadcaster; founder, *On The Line Media*

Beautiful and important work. A chorus of defiance and courage, this searing poetry collection decries the appalling subjugation of Iranian people, especially women and girls. At times blazing, at times contained, these poems sing invocations from the page for the dignity and freedom of all human beings, tenderly mixing longing for the usurped beauty and lost history of homeland with rage and grief. In a world that increasingly feels insane and full of despair, this book reminds us that we are not powerless, that reading is an act of protest, solidarity, and revolution.

—**Jane Muschenetz**, winner, California Press Women Communications Prize in Creative Verse, author of *All the Bad Girls Wear Russian Accents*

A beautiful book that illustrates the struggles of Iranian women and their decades-long battle to gain basic freedoms. There is much strength and truth in every magnificent poem.

—**Marina Nemat**, author of *Prisoner of Tehran* and *After Tehran*

Does poetry matter in the face of injustice and unspeakable violence against women? The poets of *Woman Life Freedom: Poems for the Iranian Revolution* say yes. Read these passionate, searing accounts of resistance to the state's oppression, and be moved by the young Iranians who took to the streets, paying for their dreams of freedom and equality for women with their lives. You will not be able to look away from these poems. A really, really fantastic collection. What a tour de force. Everyone should read it.

—**Julie Rak**, Professor and HM Tory Chair, University of Alberta, author of *False Summit: Gender in Mountaineering NonFiction*

An extraordinary collection of powerful poetry celebrating the brave women leading Iran's Woman, Life, Freedom revolution and mourning those who have lost their lives and their freedom. This collection of revolutionary poetry is an astonishing contribution to women's liberation worldwide. A must read for any feminist, especially those of us who might feel that we are living our lives so differently. The rights of women are under attack around the world: poetry is a remarkable instrument in solidarity with this struggle.

—**Judy Rebick**, a leader of Canada's pro-choice struggle and former president of Canada's largest women's group; educator, author of six books, most recently *Heroes in My Head*

It seems absurd to have to say it, but women's voices deserve to be heard. And women should be able to express themselves without fear of violence. And yet there are places in our world where those basic rights are systematically suppressed in pursuit of a warped idea of holiness. That's why this collection is necessary: to remind us not to take these voices for granted, and to assert without equivocation that women's voices are replete with holiness and yearning for freedom. Summoned by the intrepid Bänoo Zan and Cy Strom, the poets assembled here—local and translated, veteran and newcomer—harmonize a dynamic song on behalf of the silenced women of Iran, a song of rage, grief, empathy, and hope.

—**Adam Sol**, poet, author of *How a Poem Moves: A Field Guide for Readers of Poetry*

WOMAN LIFE FREEDOM

POEMS FOR THE IRANIAN REVOLUTION

ESSENTIAL ANTHOLOGIES SERIES 19

Canada Council for the Arts
Conseil des Arts du Canada

ONTARIO ARTS COUNCIL
CONSEIL DES ARTS DE L'ONTARIO
an Ontario government agency
un organisme du gouvernement de l'Ont

Ontario

Canada

Guernica Editions Inc. acknowledges the support of the Canada Council for the Arts and the Ontario Arts Council. The Ontario Arts Council is an agency of the Government of Ontario.

We acknowledge the financial support of the Government of Canada.

WOMAN LIFE FREEDOM

POEMS FOR THE IRANIAN REVOLUTION

EDITED BY BÄNOO ZAN AND CY STROM

GUERNICA EDITIONS

TORONTO—CHICAGO—BUFFALO—LANCASTER (U.K.)

2025

Guernica Founder, Antonio D'Alfonso

Michael Mirolla, general editor
Bänoo Zan and Cy Strom, editors
Cover and interior design: Errol F. Richardson
Cover illustration: Mohammad Sabokro

Guernica Editions Inc.
1241 Marble Rock Rd., Gananoque (ON), Canada K7G 2V4
2250 Military Road, Tonawanda, N.Y. 14150-6000 U.S.A.
www.guernicaeditions.com

Distributors:
Independent Publishers Group (IPG)
600 North Pulaski Road, Chicago IL 60624
University of Toronto Press Distribution (UTP)
5201 Dufferin Street, Toronto (ON), Canada M3H 5T8

First edition.
Printed in Canada.

Legal Deposit – First Quarter
Library of Congress Catalog Card Number: 2024948640
Library and Archives Canada Cataloguing in Publication
Title: Woman life freedom : poems for the Iranian revolution / edited by Bänoo Zan and Cy Strom.
Other titles: Woman life freedom (Guernica)
Names: Zan, Bänoo, editor. | Strom, Cy, 1954- editor.
Series: Essential anthologies series ; 19.
Description: Series statement: Essential anthologies series ; 19
Identifiers: Canadiana 20240478754 | ISBN 9781771839723 (softcover)
Subjects: LCSH: Protest movements—Iran—History—21st century—Poetry. | LCSH: Feminism—Iran—History—21st century—Poetry. | LCSH: Women's rights—Iran—History—21st century—Poetry. | LCSH: Women—Iran—Social conditions—21st century—Poetry. | LCSH: Women—Political activity—Iran—History—21st century—Poetry. | LCGFT: Poetry.
Classification: LCC PR1228 .W66 2025 | DDC 821/.9208035220955—dc23

To the martyrs of freedom

Contents

Introduction 15

BEGINNINGS

Anindita Mukherjee
sclera 25
Giovanna Riccio
You Know Me 26
Yvonne Blomer
A scarf around my hair: wimple, veil, hijab, chador, titchel, mantilla, muzzle 29
Tanis MacDonald
When the Morality Police Show Up, They Look So Familiar 31
Rasha Barrage
She reads a fairy tale 32
Laura Sheahen
Pashtun Marriage Contract 34
Kate Marshall Flaherty
The Place with a Name She Could Not Say 36
Nilou Doust
Buzz 38

DEFIANCE

Diana Woodcock
Writing to Survive 45
Dana Serea
The Rug 47
Siavash Saadlou
Woman, Life, Liberty 48
Noor Jafari
You'll try to summarize the story 50

Davood Bayat, translated by *Ali Asadollahi*
The Name 51
Mahdi Ganjavi
For the sake of "for" itself 52
Leila Farjami
The Mouth 53
Nilofar Shidmehr
Say Her Name: Mahsa Jina Amini 56

STRUGGLE

Katerina Vaughan Fretwell
One Young Life 61
Kate Marshall Flaherty
Martyrs' Square Subway Station, Tehran 62
Rasha Barrage
From dawn to dusk 65
Leila Farjami
The End Without an End 68
Razia Karimi, translated by *Ali Abdollahi* and *Theresa Rüger*
Echoes of Captive Tulips 70
Leila Farjami
Louder than These Bullets 73
Siavash Saadlou
Homeland 75
Summer Brenner
Afterwards 78
Ala Khaki
Veil Not 80
Alireza Adine, translated by *Ali Asadollahi*
Our Protests' Reality 82
Ari Honarvar
Don't Tell Mom 84
Bänoo Zan
Urgent Report 85

WITNESS

Mary Gomez Fonseca
To Mahsa: From a Painter in Solidarity 91
Ehab Lotayef
Jin – Jiyan – Azadî 92
Donna Langevin
Birdshot 93
Ayda Niknami
the pomegranate 94
Hollay Ghadery
I'm not supposed to be talking about this 96
Summer Brenner
Beautiful Stranger 97
Elana Wolff
We felt like wearing orange sports caps 98
Tanis MacDonald
Trace of Life 99
Afsar Marefat, translated by *Ari Honarvar*
Even the pavement weeps 100
Parastu Kamangir (Chang Shih Yen)
A Ghazal: Don't Forget Me 101
Mansour Noorbakhsh
Make It a Rhyme 102

FUTURES

Sheida Mohamadi, translated by *Mojdeh Bahar*
My Feverish Bed Will Hallucinate Your Body 107
Fereshteh Molavi
Zhina 111
Rahil Najafabadi
When the World Moved On Without Me 112
Azita Sadri
Fire 113

Kate Marshall Flaherty
Seven Shades of Rage 115
Bänoo Zan
She Said, He Said 117

Afterword 123

Contributors 128
Acknowledgements 134

Introduction

*Poetry and Struggle**

Poetry belongs to the world and to all of us.

A poem takes human language and wrings it out until what is left is essential expression. Words of poetry are to be recited and remembered.

The Iranian revolution that began in September 2022 responded to no political manifesto. Instead, it flared up to an unforgettable line of people's poetry: the slogan *Zan Zendegi Azadi!*—in the original Kurdish version, *Jin Jian Azadî!* Three words: Woman Life Freedom.

Within days, the Woman Life Freedom revolution also found its anthem. Amidst Persian-language reworkings of the World War II partisan song "Bella Ciao" (which kept its wildly incongruous Italian refrain), and of the 1970s Chilean insurgent chant "El Pueblo Unido Jamás Será Vencido," a string of found poetry began to sound, artfully arranged and set to music by singer-songwriter Shervin Hajipour. The people in the streets quickly taught themselves to sing this winding melody, which begins as a murmur but gathers force until a last intake of breath pushes out the words *Azadi! Azadi!*

Hajipour assembled the words of this song, which he called "Baraye," from people's tweets: some were political slogans, some were complaints, some were sweet dreams. The song gained 40 million views in 48 hours and earned Hajipour seven days in prison, with the promise of more to come. And it came.

In February 2023 "Baraye" also earned Hajipour the first ever Grammy awarded for the best song for social change.

Azadi! Azadi!

The link between poetry and struggle is nothing new in Iran.

Picture this image: "Tulips Bloom from Youths' Blood." This is the title of a poem written by Aref Qazvini (1882–1934) for Iran's Constitutional Revolution of 1906. Later set to music, in the national memory it still represents that revolution's dashed hopes. Yet its words also promise

* Portions of this introduction have appeared previously in *Asymptote Journal* and *WordCity Literary Journal.*

renewed hope with every springtime and every new generation. On a late September day in 2023, the one-year anniversary of Mahsa Jina Amini's murder, hundreds of marchers assembled in downtown Toronto, carrying posters with the photos of dead Iranian protestors against a white background. Red droplets show against this white background—they appear to be falling to the ground. And as they fall, these drops of blood spring up as stylized red tulips in the lower register of the posters. The words of Qazvini's poem have arced over more than a century and returned in 2023 as a visual on a series of protest posters.

The chants and slogans that have been called out on the streets and in the squares of Iran and across the globe are themselves a kind of poetry of the masses. In the heat of the struggle they motivate activists, pass on messages, proclaim solidarity—and construct solidarity where once it was hard to find. They raise morale, stoke emotion and publicize the cause. These chants are an artistic performance of revolt, for when people chant in the streets they are performing a people's art form at the same time as they are performing the act of revolt.

But that is not all. Looking up from the streets into the writer's study, we can find the works of poets of all lands and languages whom we know as revolutionary writers. Their words have reshaped mass struggle as personal expression, and have moulded experience into thought and word and form, and into feeling. Read, recited and sung, their words reveal the power of artistic creation to shape and propel awareness and action. And once all is done and spoken for, the art remains as witness and testimonial.

In the fall of 2022, Bänoo Zan conceived of this anthology, and we sent out the call for submissions a few months later, as winter was giving way to spring. We were looking for poems that themselves would somehow join in the struggle being waged by the women of Iran, for voices that might call back and forth across uneasy borders and proclaim transnational solidarity. Our call was answered by poets from around the world writing in many languages. The poems in this volume were written when the revolution in Iran was under way: when its course was still unknown, but its outcome was not in doubt.

What Is Poetry "for" a Revolution?

We sent out our call hoping to bring in poems that spring out of the present moment. We expected to find denunciations of injustice, laments for the fallen and bitter curses. We expected prayers, examinations of the poets' own consciences, celebrations of life, lyrical musings, autobiographical fragments and visions of a better future. We wanted this collection to uncover the dimensions of the Iranian revolution and the meaning it has for the people of Iran and the whole world.

The poets who sent us their work have not disappointed these reckless expectations. What you are reading is a book in the shape of a revolution.

But what does a book of poems do *for* a revolution? Does it somehow participate? Does it mark the occasion? Bear witness? Lend a hand? We know that when the conditions for a revolution are not realized on the ground, its goals will not be achieved. Outside the borders of Iran, we are (mostly) spectators. We watch as others take to the streets and we hold our breath. Away from the streets there may be still others whose names and faces we don't know, and who are doing the necessary work. We are not these people. But we have seen that this anthology is starting to bring together a community of creators and readers whose support for this revolution goes beyond the borders of Iran—because this feminist revolution is a beacon for the human race.

We can no longer imagine a working democratic government anywhere on earth where one-half of the population are second-class citizens and leadership positions are reserved by law and custom for men. And we can't imagine a benevolent and humane society that marginalizes its women. Or even a workable society.

Nor can the people of Iran. Forty-five years after the revolution that led to the Islamic Republic, a large part of Iran's population has had enough. The regime has lost its legitimacy—its aims and ideals no longer ring true with the people, and its systems and methods don't serve any desirable purpose for them.

The sudden, massive outbreak of the Woman Life Freedom revolution in September 2022 is the proof. Much of what took place on the streets of Iran—the chants, the demonstrations, the exuberant performance of defiance—was captured on video. The entire world saw the bravery of the people and the cruelty of the oppressor. What we witnessed excited our admiration and, as the events played out, they struck us with pity and terror.

The world also saw how this revolution unleashed a torrent of creativity. But the words that accompanied these acts were lost on those of us who do not understand the protestors' language.

This is no impediment to the creative mind. It is in the nature of the dreamer and the poet to imagine people and situations into being, to recreate protagonist and situation, and to furnish their creations with motive and conscience, fear and courage, hope and ambition. To give their imagined personae hearts and minds and histories. And it is in the nature of the arts to document lightning-quick events and extinguished lives in words that live on in hearts and minds and imaginations.

Some say that powerful works of art have incited populations to take action, and that they have changed the course of events. This claim is often made for poetry. Alongside that we might recall that there are events that have shaped the peoples of the world but are known to us only through those peoples' great epics. This still does not settle the question of whether the arts can truly shape events on their own terms, or whether social facts themselves give shape to the culture and the art (even the dissident art). But no one questions the power of the word.

Oppressors and reactionaries of all kinds hate and fear it.

Why This Book?

We launched this international anthology to discover new voices and to bring into being a virtual community whose engagement will be transformed into activism.

The cause of freedom has long depended on the arts to give it voice. Words that are spoken may be forgotten, and books of essays lie unopened on the shelf, but lines of poetry live and speak forever. In the urgency of the moment, this book marks the events as they unfold; its voices echo that urgency and will carry it on to reach other minds in far-off places.

This book bears witness to a world-historical event: the first ever feminist revolution. In Iran, poetry is a national treasure—imagine a culture that has six Shakespeares (or more), as far as stature of the poets and familiarity with their lines is concerned. These are great poets whose lines are loved and recited by heart. It is fitting to dedicate a collection of poems as an offering to the women of Iran and to their struggle.

We want the poets and the people of Iran to know that their voices are heard beyond their borders. We want the poems in this anthology to speak the words that trouble oppressors. We intend this to be a book of poetry that captures the moment … and lives on.

We want to demonstrate to the world that this cause is alive and will not be put down.

The Poems

We thank every one of the poets who answered the call we put out and entrusted their works to us. We read and evaluated all submissions "blind" with no knowledge of any poet's name, identity or place of origin.

We believe that the poems in the following pages breathe authenticity and urgency. They deserve their place in this volume of poems for the Iranian revolution.

After we had made our choice of poems to include we discovered that the authors and translators of these poems have varied origins and live in many different countries. This is as it should be. Iran's Woman Life Freedom revolution lit a spark that will continue to flare up around the world. No one population or culture is the only victim of the oppressor, the only body engaged in the struggle. Those who see these events and refuse to turn away have seen that this is not someone else's cause.

If we cannot all be direct participants, we can be witnesses.

Witness is one of the outstanding themes in this collection. Some of the poems might persuade readers that the poet was an eyewitness to the events on the streets of Iran. That may be true. The act of witness in this group of poems is written as hard reality—the pity and the terror they evoke are almost too hard to bear. Other poems achieve a laser-sharp outsider perspective. Whoever they are and whatever their histories and trajectories, these are poets whose works take up the struggle alongside the women of Iran even while they appear to acknowledge distance and strangeness.

Yes, distance and strangeness—not exoticism. It is no easy matter to perform this act of solidarity without sounding a whole symphony of false notes. We are fortunate to have found poems written by Western poets who took this leap across cultures and were able to persuade us with their genuineness and clarity of vision.

What about Iranians living in Western lands? Many of these poets imagine themselves living their (relatively, contingently) liberated lives in two phases: living freely (here, or possibly even there), and bound by harsh restrictions (there, or even here). The result is a double vision that sets up an aching division of the self in the poem. Keeping a wary eye on the society while looking inward is another kind of witness.

Sometimes the act of witness seems to confound the witnesses themselves and comes out as a dream state or hallucination, a surreal landscape of the mind. Readers may find among these poems versions of the Iran of ancient myth, in which the myths are upended and a veil is ripped open to reveal glimpses of the disturbing present.

There are also works of plain defiance in this collection. Some of them read like song lyrics or call out slogans like an anthem or a march, a rousing revolutionary call. What could contrast more strongly with these than those soul-searching poems where the writer trembles before the need to act heroically, or even to bear witness, all too often arriving at a doubt that there is no way to resolve? Yet these too are poems *for* the revolution which, if we are honest with ourselves, we know must mobilize both leader and follower, the one who is certain and the one who is less certain, the hero and the rest of us.

Cy Strom
Toronto
July 2024

BEGINNINGS

Anindita Mukherjee

sclera

none of them
resemble their faces—
Black veil of veils

Giovanna Riccio
You Know Me

Over the decades women have increasingly
pushed back, particularly in the big cities
wearing their headscarves far back on their heads (Al Jazeera)

You know me as Mahsa, but in truth, doubly blessed
daughter of Wisdom's warrior goddess, Anahita
and my natural mother, I portend life
my name a worldly Kurdish word
sounding earth's rooted echo.

Each dawn, the heavens teemed with untamed birdsong
while Mother's tintinnabulation chimed in my ears,
a no-hiatus prophecy drummed by thumping batons
or music enslaved by councils of codgers engraving
edicts on female flesh: *Jina-girl*
Please—veil those fey straying locks
tame your feral thoughts or brimstone cops
may misread youthful pluck for scorn

Disciple of motherlove
I'd comb, cajole and plait my snarly mane:
twine *please* into *yes*, braid a nod to a daughterly kiss,
I'd gather, toss, pinch'n rally my hijab, but dissenting strands
craved air, succumbed to the fly-aways, braved
free-floating static electricity sabotaging mullahs' commands.
Though I gelled and lacquered, moussed and pinned,
mutinous tresses strayed into Shamal winds
tugged, caressed, slapped unbridled air spirited
as Peshmerga freedom-fighters.

Mark this photo of mom, dad and me strolling with Kiarash,
in trendy ebony gear—a cosmopolitan woman
chancing the headstrong highjinks of the open sky
my hijab's half-hearted, set back so illicit locks halo my face.

Craving big-city suavité, I bared a single plait, dared
rouged lips and kohled eyes   stepped soulful, weightless
as flute-boned laughing doves arabesquing Tehran's sky
'til highlighted good-looks pinned me
in the bleeding glare of Morality's roving toughs,
thin-men who police all who deny them love.

Shackled like everywoman's body, I'm caged
trucked, to a *briefing class*, for *re-education*—
a reiteration of Ayatollah's Allah-usurping thunder
merging wilful dress with blasphemous nudity—
no less.

For risking liberty's flair, my bully-sticked mouth's
crimsoned with gory lipstick, smile pulped.

Now mark this second portrait:
my hair, scarf-free on waxen hospital linens

View omens in tubes assaulting
my mouth, nose, arteries until the dawn *Amins*
and Guardians sign Jina as death's epithet.

exponential in raucous streets
you, Life's essential poets
you who unflinching
may falter yet, convinced
the woman I seek has become death.

And you, Woman
torching hijabs into suns
reversing my adieu
translate Mahsa into Freedom

Not so I am become YOU

Shamal: north, in Persian
Mahsa Amini's Kurdish name, Jina, means "life."

Yvonne Blomer

A scarf around my hair: wimple, veil, hijab, chador, titchel, mantilla, muzzle

Worn down. Worn out. Worn in.
It's ok, women are not worn
thin by all the men, male, master, macho,
manful, mannish, manlike, paternal,
he-man, dude, chap, feller, fellow, guy.
No. Not worn out. No, we're fine.
Just raped. Whatever. Just jailed,
dragged from the street for our—
what's that, women? Your bare-head-as-immoral-
behavior while sister's forced to marry at 13?—
Not worn down. Worn out. Worn in.
You know, dressing or not dressing,
covering up or not covering up. Being too
hidden—remember police dragging women
in Burkinis off French beaches for being too
shielded? No, we're not worn thin.
Nope, not us. We're womaning up.
Tired? Not even. Forget it!
We're just starting again.
Just getting started, again. Again
we're getting started. Again and again.
Volleyballers forced into bikinis
where men wear board shorts.
Are we mad? Nope. More like inured,
angry, irate, ballistic, rabid, pissed,
ticked, shirty, rankled, fuming, sore, bruised
from beach rash and thrown rocks.
Bombs, guns, weapons aren't immoral at all?
Women, we're just waving this flag,
call it #metoo, call it #womanlifefreedom.

We're different, each woman, it's true,
but we bleed the same: red, pain.
Sometimes we go out just to go out—
not to be seen, especially, just to be
female, lady, girl, lass, lassie,
gal, sister, femme, broad, Ms., Miss.
Nope, we're not worn thin. Not worn out. Not
tired. Scared or scarred, sure,
maybe a little terrified, let's face it. It's a lot.
Something from the 70s, Roe vs Wade, gone.
In 1936 Iran had "the great
unveiling." Enforced not to then, enforced to
now. Then, protected by police if they didn't.
Now, beaten by police if they don't.
That's ok. I can't keep track either.
Are you taking notes? Have you got this
being woman thing
figured out? That's ok. Just tie that silk
scarf around your mouth (scream therein),
breathe as if you are acceptable, tolerable,
legalized, approved, endorsed, legitimate, allowed.

Tanis MacDonald

When the Morality Police Show Up, They Look So Familiar

Like the student who frowns as I speak, leans
against my classroom wall, chin up, crossed arms

like the student who wants me to dress
more modestly, disappointed when I don't

like the student who fills his exam booklet
with drawings of a dick and balls

like the man who asks if he can register for
my women's literature class, and when I say of course,

he furrows his brow and says *but then I'd have*
to read all these books by women

and you would grade me
on what I wrote about women

when the morality police show up
I recognize them all

Rasha Barrage

She reads a fairy tale

A [child] must not travel without the consent of [their parents].

A [child] can be married at the age of thirteen, or younger, with the consent of a judge. They must relinquish their dolls, toys, and dreams, and surrender their body to acts that their mind cannot conceive.

A [child] must not engage in activities that are against the family values of [their parents].

A [child] may be smacked, kicked, punched, and hurtled across a room, if a [parent] commands it.

But. The [child] must not be a boy. Not a brother.

But a girl in pigtails. A woman. Your sister.

And the world watches, in the name of sovereignty.

A girl of nine years, who skips to school and laughs with the clouds. She does not cry. The girl does not weep.

She is Cinderella. She is Moana. She is Elsa. She rises still, while the adults watch in their sleep.

And the world whispers in dissent.

The little princess loses her crown as she bleeds. Becoming a vessel for an old man's ambition. A chasm. A valley. A pit of lies that society sewed generations before, when her grandmothers' and aunties' glass slippers became glued to the floor. She does not cry. The girl does not weep.

And the world sobs with words of condemnation.

She gathers signatures, while the kings play at being men. The princess, she rises and wrenches the beards from their façade. Thread by tiny thread, she extracts each little hair from its root. In silence, she reads and threads.

A [child] can feel the violent searing agony that makes them scream the scream of a thousand soldiers. A foetus can crack the premature hips and cause fourth degree tears to the body parts of a [child] that must not be named.

And the world believes a girl must endure such fate.

The kings create fabrications, they weave society as a scarf that strangles its princess.

But. She plucks, plucks, plucks away with every breath of her being. Her mother murmurs in her dreams, the eggs she planted in the princess's body dancing with vibrations of defiance.

A girl of nine years. She gathers all her sisters. Her citizens and cousins. The scientists and artists.

The little princess and her kin. They soak their sweat into the soil and sprout words for their daughters. The girls yet to come, who will feel murmurs beneath their feet. Who will find shards of glass emblazoned with blood.

The signatures were not names, but a story after all. One word, and one strand at a time. A girl in pigtails uttered words that shredded the hair from the kings.

And the world heard the echoes of "Woman, Life, Freedom".
Shaking the earth and unrelenting.
Finally, the pretence stopped.
The princess was the ending.

Laura Sheahen

Pashtun Marriage Contract

Our wedding day
my father signed:
Flesh is for you
but the bones are mine.

From moon to moon
red bruises shine
Flesh is for you
the bones are mine.

Black lash for blood
brown lash to bind
Flesh is for you
the bones are mine.

Our daughters watch
our small son whines
Flesh is for you
the bones are mine.

No fractures, breaks,
the terms defined:
Flesh is for you
but the bones are mine.

Where I will go
you will not find—

The flayed skin gone,
this stays behind:

The flesh was yours

My bones are mine.

When I was traveling in Afghanistan for an NGO, I heard that this line was included in marriage agreements: a husband was permitted to beat his wife but not break her bones.

Kate Marshall Flaherty

The Place with a Name She Could Not Say

at Brottier Refugee Resettlement House, 1993

Her voice was soft through the thin reed of her body,
her scarlines showed in the hallway to the shower.
In my second pregnancy we lived together
at Brottier House. Nights my daughter slept in her crib,
we sat on the balcony, under the stars, whispering
stories of that place.

University, they called it,
the cells for students. Lines burned
onto flesh to stop words,
welt-stripes like prison bars.

She was there, the place with the name
she could not say—
just mouthed the word, *Evin* prison,
rhymes with *heaven*, but
stings of tear gas, and flesh cuts like hellfire.

Maryam came through La Casa,
escaped the Shah, SAVAK, somehow,
and Tehran's terror beside a tea house.
Hoped for a house of refuge, here, where she crisped
oiled rice tops into sweet crust,
made strongest chai, sang purring Farsi laments.

She danced with our toddler,
we learned signs for *happy*—
bird wisp hands up on the chest—
and small curl of two fingers on the palm for *earth*,
our tilted planet.

Who am I to write of my friend,
and that place,
something smashed down, welled up,
that must be named.

Brottier House: Operated by the Spiritan Order as a non-profit to assist private sponsors in welcoming refugees to Canada. The poet lived at 63 Hambly Avenue, Toronto, the original Brottier Refugee Resettlement House, as a volunteer from 1992 to 1994 with her husband and two children.

La Casa: Founded in 1984 by women of the Catholic Diocese of Buffalo, NY, to assist asylum seekers from Central and South America. Asylum seekers were housed at convents until one of these was converted into a housing facility called Vive La Casa, currently located in Buffalo.

SAVAK: Secret intelligence organization of Iran established by the Shah in 1957 and disbanded in 1979.

"terror beside a teahouse": Evin Prison is located in the district known as Evin; a large park with a popular upscale teahouse and restaurant is immediately next to it. It is illegal to photograph the prison's surroundings.

Nilou Doust
Buzz

My mom swats away a fly I didn't realize had been nesting on my scarf.

"I'm too hot. I want to wear shorts."
Her eyes stare straight ahead. She says nothing.

"Hey! You two! You better be related. Respect the Quran, you pieces of shit."
My best friend lets go of my hand.
Then he's on the floor.

My screams don't sound like they're mine.

"Mom, they told me I need to wear a hijab to be a big girl."
I'm nine years old when they tell me that my body

is too enticing.

That the braids my mother's fingers worked into my hair
will make grown men want to fuck me.

I'm in first grade.

I fidget with clay on my desk.
"As young women, you should think of yourself as a chocolate bar.
Left unwrapped, flies will swarm.
Keep yourself covered."

The pink rimmed head scarf of the first graders is too tight around my neck.

They tell me:

"Men can't control themselves."

The man I call my uncle, my best friend from preschool,
Their hands are now weapons, ridden with disease.

I'm seven years old, half listening, worried about my doll not having a hijab.

I can hear buzzing.

They tell me:

"You're going to go to hell."

I'm eighteen years old.
Where I live now, the skies are blue,
and my legs and arms are tanned and scarred.

Uncovered.
Flies swarm.

I'm in a boy's bed. He pushes my hair out of my face.

"You two better be related."
I can hear the screams as if they were mine.

Pray for Iran. Stand up for Iran.

Kids my age,
dead,
dead,
dead.

My eyes stare straight ahead. I do nothing.

I cry over the boy who pushed my hair out of my face.
In another life my eyes are rimmed from exhaustion,
restless and focused.
"Freedom or Death!"

In this life, my eyes stare straight ahead. I do nothing.

DEFIANCE

Diana Woodcock

Writing to Survive

She would survive, refusing
to wallow in grief—her beliefs
in altruism, humanity,
peace and poetry would keep
her alive. Writing, her escape,
set her free long before the door
of her prison cell was unlocked.

She did not break.
The sensory deprivation,
constant interrogations,
accusations and humiliations
turned her into a patient stone.

From the scenes she witnessed
through the sliver of window
not covered by metal, she drew hope—
a thistle pushing up out of the pavement,
a sparrow taking flight. And she wrote:
I said to myself,
Are you less than a weed then?
And … I felt a surge of the sap
of spirit blaze within.

Her verses smuggled out
of Tehran's Evin Prison make
me weep. Lacking recrimination,
they are fashioned out of compassion.
By writing, she survived.
She immortalized all the women
who have died in prison,
stuffed into bags, nameless.

What saved her through an eternal
decade in prison—what gave
her strength—was simply
and purely writing poetry,
        the most dangerous
        act of resistance.

In 2017, Iranian poet Mahvash Sabet won the PEN Pinter International Writer of Courage Award. Her book, translated into English, is *Prison Poems* (George Ronald, 2013).

The patient stone, in Persian idiom, is one who absorbs suffering, carries its burden, and endures.

Dana Serea

The Rug

Start by making the warps out of cotton yarn,
beginning the long weave of history.
Loop in the wefts, strings of pain and sorrow.
Make sure the color is red, the color of eliminated families,
their blood dripping down the long tapestry.
Twist in the memories of the disappeared,
the victims erased by the government.
Tie in the knots of the events
and remember the thousands of lives:
A knot for my neighbor's daughter, kidnapped by the secret police
and never seen again. A knot for the woman
shot by a military guard for protesting in the streets,
her cries for liberty silenced by the regime.
A knot for the people forced into exile.
A knot for the bodies never found.
A knot for the women abused and beaten by the police.
Finish the weave with fringes of innocent deaths,
intertwining with the memory of the country's grim past.
Hang it on the wall, a daily reminder
of the ones who died. For the ones who survived.

Siavash Saadlou

Woman, Life, Liberty

for Jina (Mahsa) Amini

You had left your hometown—
your very own Kurdistan—to visit
the cursed capital of a nation blighted
by some benighted men who took you
away, with your brother begging, saying
that the two of you had no one, that the
two of you were *ghareeb* in this monster
of a city we call Tehran, where the strands
of your hair became the biggest thorn in
the side of this regime ravenous for
rooting out all the young voices, failing
to fathom that *you can't burn women made of fire.*

I left Iran, worried that my words
would atrophy under the auspices
of the Ayatollah. My mother's tears
bled into the water she had
poured on the floor as we said our
final goodbyes late at night, when
you must have been fast asleep,
dreaming what any twenty-two-year-old
would dream when the pictures in
their head scamper away from
the prying hands of tyranny.

Planeload after planeload of us
Iranians flee Iran for places where
inquisitive faces await us on every
street corner, at every store and
every coffee shop. What do I tell
these people about your crime?
Mahsa *jaan*, Mahsa *gian*—what do I say
when they ask, "What did they kill her for?"

I tell them: Her name was Mahsa.
She loved liberty. She loved life.
She was vivacious. Her crime?
Exuding light in a land ruled by darkness.

A version of this poem was first published in *Porter House Review*, Texas State University, April 2023.

Ghareeb is a word meaning "stranger" used by way of plea by Mahsa Amini's brother at the time of their arrest, asking the Morality Cops to let the two of them go.

Jaan is a word meaning "life" in Persian, used as a term of endearment. Likewise, *gian* means "life" in Kurdish, and is used as a term of endearment.

Noor Jafari

You'll try to summarize the story

into a fairytale. In this story
two girls fall in love
in college and they're roommates.
In this story the girls go to pretty cafés,
hold hands in their dorm as the sunset
reflects pink-ish orange on their cheeks
that are already pink from laughing,
and the sunset, though beautiful, adds
nothing to this scene. But in this story,
in this country, the girls go to the park
only after dark. This story will be
posted on Twitter before being replaced
by a public apology from the girls.
You wonder if their alibi is strong enough.
You wonder if, before they were caught,
the girls got a chance to hold hands,
to feel each other's palm sweating.
How simple it would be for you
to hold hands with a girl, to feel her pulse
against yours, to notice her eyes
change color in the sun. This story
may not be worth reading
if you're looking for an ending,
but you will summarize it
into a story about love.

Davood Bayat
translated by Ali Asadollahi
The Name

The epitaph on Jina Amini's grave:
Jina, dear! You will not die. Your name will turn into a SYMBOL

The garden is called the garden
The flower is yet the flower and it's called the flower
The tree, though cut down, is called the tree
The cities called the cities, and the street the street
just like darkness in the daylight that is still darkness
History is called history despite repetitions
Objects and things are called objects and things
If bullets rain, it won't be called rain, it's called bullets
The far sea is the far sea and the bright star, even in dusty air, is a bright star
Destiny is still called destiny and the dream is still the dream
Nothing has changed, nothing will be named twice
There is only courage
with numerous names, and heroes with indistinct faces
Each has lost a life and gained a name
a name whose glory echoes in heavens
and gently asks:
Say the *SYMBOL-word*
that this door may open
that it may begin

Mahdi Ganjavi

For the sake of "for" itself

For saving the words from the school walls,
For the farewell party that emerged from the depths of fear,
For the fearful glance of my friend from behind the door; from within his eyes,
For the boy who was set at the head of the line to recite the Qur'an, yet also sought to read everyone's body in the school bus,
For the Arabic teacher whose hand was longer than the children's waists,
For my ears, leased to your words in every city park,
For the fantasies bent to fit the confines of your expectations,
For the erstwhile naïve classmate turned into your cheap ideological mouthpiece,
For the fear that dissipated our shared memories,
For the dread of police, motorcycles, eavesdropping, and doorbells,
For gazing at Evin prison from the university's hillside dormitory,
For assessing the odds of captivity before the pursuit of discovery,
For the furrowed brow of writing etched upon the tablet of "chain murders,"
For the undisclosed fears of the loved ones,
Because your method entrenches scattered anxieties,
For paranoia, suspicion of classmates, fellow citizens, and guests,
For state-sanctioned conflicts in the name of love,
For your authority in defining the limits of the body,
For our vulnerable, homeless, and manipulated dignity,
For attempting to forget the relentless barrage of nonsense,
For the ideological webs spun around every fragment of poetry,
To safeguard Rumi, Hafez and Sa'di from coercion's grasp,
For incessantly breathing in religious smog,
For the waters you've desiccated,
For the debased languages,
To evade the spiritual police baton,
For the celebrities of hypocrisy,
To champion the cause,
for the sake of "for" itself.

Leila Farjami

The Mouth

I

Beware!

The plainclothes men are watching.

No one dares scribble your name
on plaster-peeled walls of this town.

You strolled these streets, narrow, quaint,
walked the alleys teeming
with stray cats and passersby,
greeted the baker, fruit vendor, butcher,
second-hand jeweler, seamstress who sewed
your wedding dress—never worn.

On winter's last day,
with your hair tousling,
draping your cheek,

you watered the night-blooming jasmine,

pruned the apricot boughs
clawing the windowpane,

harvested the ripening walnuts—creamy flesh
rounded in green moons,
inking the fingers—
dehusked grains of rice, pot-ready,
baked a cake
for your baby brother's birthday.

II

Why you were arrested:

indecent coverage in a public space
per Sharia Law—
a half-slipped veil on your head,
fully clothed.
Sentenced to eighty lashes
for defying the dress code, compulsory.

Your eyelid eclipsed,
jaw broken,
neck bruised.

After prison release
your body was a land, plundered,
heaped in amorphous blues,
purples.

This is you.
The woman who unearths voices,
rubbled.

All day long
people chant,
Zan, Zendegi, Azadi!
Woman, Life, Freedom!

III

Together we shoulder the bodies
of our sisters shrouded in cotton cloths,
march toward the graveled ditches
dug in rows—
wombs gaping,
unmarked.

Chrysanthemums wilting,
trampled in slush and mud,
mired white.

The blood streaming on your temple
is the last we saw
of your face.

On the way home,
darkness melds with streetlights blown out,
black—monster's missing teeth—

the mouth
we flee,
dying.

Nilofar Shidmehr

Say Her Name: Mahsa Jina Amini

Speak it boldly, let it resound
with such force that the stagnant
air is stirred, compelling veils to fall away,
and women's locks to cascade freely,
draping over their shoulders as they unite
in town squares, dancing around
bonfires, igniting the flames of liberty
by burning their hijabs.

Say Her Name:
Declare it loudly, louder than the politicians' lengthy
speeches, with a pitch higher than
their grand podiums; proclaim her name above
the watchtowers of prisons, and more confidently
than the authoritarian commands
of pressure groups, riot police, Basijis, informants,
and with greater intensity than the volley of gunfire;
shout her name louder than the sniper fire from rooftops;
call her name louder than the fear sown
by the ongoing purges and the fresh
graves for protesters and dissidents.
Let her name resonate so distinctly
that it transforms into an irresistible
chant for freedom.

Say Her Name:
Repeat it so fearlessly that
the winds, with their flowing tresses, will rush
to knock on the doors of a people feigning slumber,
beckoning them to step out onto the streets;
echo her name with such fervor

that her memory sparks a glimmer of hope
in people's hearts, igniting
the embers of their dream.
Like a chorus confined behind the scene,
may they emerge from the dark chambers
of isolation and embrace the blazing streets
where dancing women set fire to their veils.

Say Her Name
To the wind, akin to a traveling bard,
wandering from city to city,
village to village, playing its enticing tune
in town squares, inviting the people
to assemble once more and sing her name
with unwavering courage,
sing it with such resonant cadence
that the scattered strands of her hair gather,
intertwine, form a flag
that rises proudly in the name of
Woman Life Freedom.

STRUGGLE

Katerina Vaughan Fretwell

One Young Life

Imagine an ordinary bus ride in Tehran
could be your last.
Only sixteen, perhaps you're riding to class,
homework tucked firmly in knapsack,
text messages flying.
In a rush, you forgot to grab your hijab
or you dared to protest the female dress code.

A hand grabs your soft shoulder and you turn—
two scary men stare you down like a criminal.
Mere sight of your locks
crazes the Morality Squad. Could be their daughter.

They drag you from the bus, throw you down,
beat, bludgeon, batter you senseless,
your defenceless body shuts off,
shuts out the strong-armed tyranny
denying you breath.

What are your final, conscious thoughts?
Do you wonder who'll feed your canary
before darkness descends?
Do you grieve loved ones
before darkness descends?
Does the urge for justice bolster you
before darkness descends?

Kate Marshall Flaherty

Martyrs' Square Subway Station, Tehran

October 5, 2023

In the waiting room
I can't help
but watch the news,
magnifying—

All I see is red
cross hairs
        target—
an average morning
on the last car 134
Martyrs'
        Square

All I see—
a red circle
mute footage
in less than seconds—
Armita Geravand
slides
from standing strong
        to supine—

Hidden from all sight—
"morality" police
in seconds
        suppress

Sunday blood
pressure
pulses
to just more
        coerced
confessions—

one year
after another
        death—

Mahsa Amini—

Her name
chanted
here

while Armita lies
bandaged
in a coma
there—

their loosened silk
defiance

        a right-less law
I can't see—

        in the red circle
within seconds
women bow,

slide a prostrate body
into the spotlight

And we can't stop
saying your names—

eye witnesses'
red circle widening
        to the world—

and won't stop
        repeating your names—

Mahsa, Armita, Tahireh and *all*—

        pushing for *women*
                for life
                        for freedom

Rasha Barrage

From dawn to dusk

In 2022
The sun began its ascent
So, why does he look at me?

Dawn has risen and
God-forbid!
I see a strand of hair
What disgrace is this!
A hair
A hair!
I see the wisp of temptation
A flowing flag of freedom
A call to seduction!

He bares his teeth
A creature in desperate need of violence
Repressed, repressed
Sexual frustration at its almighty best
He is just as suppressed

A disgrace
Dishonour
A lesson must be learnt
These disgraceful young women
No shame and no honour

Undressing me,
his eyes loiter
Too long, too long
He puckers his lips and flares his nostrils in hunger

She will see who I am
What her actions deserve
These unmarried women
Flaunting their bodies for all to observe

What does he think I am?
Inanimate, a vessel?
Does he see humanity?

His uniform asphyxiates the boy in him
Forgotten and discarded
His spirit diseased with ideology

Blinded to me, to my sanctuary
I am a refuge, a reminder of his worth
Yet he only seeks supremacy

She must learn the lesson
Of humility and respect
Her mother beside her
A father humiliated by her disgrace
I will teach them all!
The family, the country—shamed by its daughters

In the dusk of freedom
Hair as black as the twilight sky
Inevitably escapes
Weaving its soft caress away from my neck
Reminding him of the stars that once made him
That blessed him into creation
How connection makes us, propels us to imagination

In the dusk of freedom, he will be free
His spirit alive to creation
For the glory of nature that can simply be

The title is inspired by the chants of protestors who participated in the 1979 demonstrations in Tehran: "In the dawn of freedom, we have no freedom." The protests were in response to the new Islamist regime's edict compelling women to wear hijabs.

Leila Farjami

The End Without an End

for Sarina Esmaeilzadeh, killed in anti-regime demonstrations in Iran on September 23, 2022

Who knew bullets could immortalize us,
make us as endless as the blood streaks
on the city boulevards?

Death hands us
a thousand wings,
a thousand skies.

In our motherland, the moon revives the decaying stars,
descends to enfold the mangled bodies in the alleys,
tends to their final sighs.

Being Eve's daughters,
bare and elemental
as water and light,
we speak the native tongue
of the shunned,
rename all dying things to revive them—
the animals,
birds,
trees.

We walk footless
from one zodiac to another,
breathe fertile air
into the infinite ether.

We make love to the wind
like banyan roots,
summon the night's flesh,
vine around its waxen darkness.

At dawn,
we are sisters
who bury the young bones of our dead,
lay white lilies
on their nameless graves,

huddle like black sparrows
in the chilling gust.

Razia Karimi
translated by Ali Abdollahi and Theresa Rüger

Echoes of Captive Tulips

Do not ask me
about the mood of my heart.

These days, it often weeps
for the sorrow of captive tulips in my homeland.
Their selves concealed,
their corpses blossom on the streets.

My days fall to dusk in tears
and my dawns break against the ceiling.

In times I forget myself,
search for hours
for my lost self
among caravans of fallen girls.

In a land so far from them, I suffer by their side.
My braided locks—
no coquette's curls—
coil around my throat, choked with sobs.

Hair that has drawn thousands like me to the gallows
and imprisoned thousands like me in a cage.

Hair that has made thousands like me
their own murderers.
Strands and curls that have taken away the right to life
from thousands like me.

Sometimes I hate my female body,
sentenced for centuries,
for centuries subjected to the judgment of fatwas.

It is stoned by the hands of the executioner,
set on fire on the street and in the mosque.

Do you have time?
To linger by my heart
and cast a glance at the beauties of my land,
and read the black sorrow of the captive
in the silence of their eyes?

Do you have time?
So that I can tell you
how withered the gardens of my homeland are,
narcissus and jasmine wilted?

It has been a long time
since the dawn carried a sweet scent.

Sepideh, the dawn, was extinguished in Taleb's grasp.
Aftaab, the sun, hanged herself
after her release from prison.
Darya, the sea, severed her veins
after her liberation.
There has been no news from Mahtab, the moonlight.
Qays went mad waiting for Layla.

Cast a glance
at the girls of my homeland,
passengers of a leaking boat
upon an ocean full of wolves.

Stay with me.
Me and the strangled voices of thousands.
The thousands like me.

Sepideh and other names in its stanza are women's names, although the legendary Qays is a man better known by his epithet Majnoon, meaning "madman." Taleb refers to the Taliban of today.

Leila Farjami
Louder than These Bullets

for Mahsa Amini, killed by the Iranian regime on September 16, 2022

Louder than these bullets
is the incantation of your name,
Mahsa!

Stars are lucent pebbles that plunge
into the earth's grey mouth.
The moon heaves,
dims its orb.
Clouds cluster like mourners,
hover with their bent heads, leaden faces
over your cold body.

In the streets
a woman burns her headscarf,
a man who hurls a stone at a militia member
gets shot,

a mother scissors off her long hair
to lay it on her daughter's grave.

In the streets
the future charges toward an open square,
screams with its blistered mouth,
Death to the dictator!

The future sings for both
the dead and the living;
it bears their blue-river souls
to a far-burgeoning sea.

Some children swear

they have seen you walking
among the chanting crowds,
running through dark alleys
to elude the armed men,
standing on the curbside
to tend to the wounded and the dying.

At last, you are free as the soil that shrouds you.

Your fingers are rooting deep
into the Saqqez riverbank,
the land of black cumin seeds,
damask roses, and torrid zephyrs.

Diaphanous, weightless,
the air carries the scent of clover and chamomile
to embalm your naked bones.

Mahsa!
Light is a rebel
born of a veiled flame,
her lithe phantom
sprouts in solitude through slits,
wounds.

Light is a mother
who breathes for her newborns.

Like you,
she merges with the horizon's magenta,
flowers into
a strange sun,

dawns at midnight.

Siavash Saadlou
Homeland

for Kian Pirfalak

Norooz is here at last, darling …
Time for yet another new beginning
harking back to a homeland I can hardly
call my own now. I sit at a coffee shop
in downtown Vancouver—the voices
intoning around me—an echo chamber.

Hard to think of the *haft-seen* arrangement,
of sprouts and oleaster, vinegar and apple
and garlic and sumac, sweet pudding, or
fortune-telling through a *Hafiz* poem—
so hard, even, to think of the pitiably short
life span of the goldfish when the face of
nine-year-old Kian Pirfalak comes to mind,
the little boy who lived in Izeh, a city in southern
Iran with hot-summer climate, where
he dreamed ("Dreamed" being the operative word)
that he would someday work for NASA, and
where he was shot and killed by security forces
    on November 15, 2022.

In a video Kian's mom has shared of her
son, he is testing his hand-made boat for
a school project, his chubby face forming
a smile as expansive as life itself.
"In the name of the God of rainbows,"
    he speaks.

The line is from a poem for third graders:
In the name of the God of rainbows,
God whose compassion only grows.

God who created colorful dragonflies,
God who conceived of gorgeous butterflies.

In Iran, the men in power steal the bodies
of those they kill, keeping the lifeless flesh
and bones hostage for days, releasing it only
if the grieving family promises they will
hold a humble funeral, without a large crowd
gathering around the grave singing laments
for a life that will never return.

The government is afraid of the living
and even more so of the dead.
"Hear it from me about how the shooting
happened," says Kian's mom at the funeral,
"so they can't say it was done by terrorists—
because they're lying."

In the name of the God of rainbows,
God whose compassion only grows.
God who created colorful dragonflies,
God who conceived of gorgeous butterflies.

At the coffee shop I hear a teenage girl
telling her company of two, after hanging
up the phone, that she believes her friend
on the other end was "fake-sleeping."
How bizarre, I think to myself, to be
thinking about a perished nine-year-old
just then.

Norooz today is not a New Day
But No – *Rooz,* the day that says,
"No"; that says, "We are still here,"
—that says—my homeland is Kian;
my homeland is Kian.

A version of this poem was first published in *Thin Air Magazine*, Northern Arizona University, May 2023.

Norooz literally means "New Day" in Persian and is a word used to refer to the Persian New Year. The lines quoted are from a poem originally written by Mohammad Purvahab and included in third-grade Persian language textbooks in Iran.

Summer Brenner
Afterwards

After they kill her they'll return her body
They'll leave her body on the step
They'll knock loudly on the door and drive away

My husband will open the door and make a sound I've never heard
The sound an animal makes when it's about to die

I will run to the front of the house and see my husband on the floor
I'll think he has had a heart attack until I see her head below his arm
Her leg below his leg and I will help him rise

Together we will carry her into the house, into the dark house of sorrow
We will lay her on her bed next to her tokens of girlhood
Her books and drawings, her purse her ring her photos

We will hold her hands of broken fingers
We will touch her face crushed on one side
We will stroke her mangled ear, her twisted mouth, her limp neck

I will bathe her white skin, her long black hair
I will sponge away the blood from the lips of her broken vagina

Later the official report will come, later the certificate of death will come
Later we will read she fell from a roof, we'll read she was run over
By a train, we'll read she took her own life

I won't remember the funeral, they'll tell me I screamed
They'll tell me I ripped my hijab and fainted
They'll tell me I tried to climb inside her grave

After the earth has covered her I will tear my clothes
I will tear at my eyes, tear out my hair
I won't eat or drink, I won't smile or laugh

Overnight I'll grow old and empty
I'll spend my waking hours cursing them and praying
I'll pray they die in agony, I'll pray they suffer
I'll pray for their death and mine

If I dare to sleep I'll have nightmares
I'll enter the torture chamber as an angel, a witness, a mother
I'll cry out in my sleep there is no consolation, I will say
There is no future, I will say

And then the day will come when I see my neighbor's child
A friend of my own child, a girl like her left broken
And abandoned on the step and I will run to help.

Ala Khaki

Veil Not

to the heroic women of Iran fighting for "Woman, Life, Freedom,"
November 10, 2022

Unveil your rage, my
sister, unveil the night.

Let the old cloaked men
who declare heaven is
beneath your feet, while they
put you in a dark well, see
your might.

Unveil your rage, my
sister, unveil the night.

Set this forsaken land
alight, with a bonfire of veils
from Caspian to the
Gulf.
Blaze away this blight.

Unveil your rage, my
sister, unveil the night.

Dispatch them to
hell. Let your fire
purge their
scourge
once and for all.

Unveil your rage, my
sister, unveil the night.

Upon the ashes
with bricks of
justice, mortar of
love, colors of
hope,
we shall build a new citadel.

Unveil your rage, my
sister, unveil the night.

Alireza Adine
translated by Ali Asadollahi

Our Protests' Reality

Not only blood …
shit spreads too
after you're shot.

It's not always like this:
that a bullct picrccs thc body
'n blood spatters. Or hits a neck
'n you shout: "Oh, look! his neck just bloomed!"

It's mostly shitty.
That's why out of every thousand names
only one's given out.
There's got to be a clean carcass on everyone's lips.
I've buried a sheep's guts myself. I know.
Makes you vomit.
Let alone a man's gut.
It turns yellow under the body;
from the holes in the intestine, just wind comes out:
The foul wind. Not that nice-smelling wind, you know. No!
But the wind blowing from a hole in the gut.

Not only blood …
I saw someone killed in a protest
'n for two hours, he was farting.
People were laughing.

This video can't be released.
If it's released, it's not just the stench that breaks out, it's the people's laughter.
'N when there's laughing,
you can't fuck the coup d'état regime in the ass.

So, it can't be released.
That's why they tell the snipers to shoot at the gut.

Clean death
comes on the air.
But there are always more dead:
More dirty death.
More killed
than they announce.

Ari Honarvar

Don't Tell Mom

Tell Mom of splashes of nasturtium on the green canvas of the lawn
Of narcissus flowers playing hide and seek with butterflies

Of girls, their hair dancing in the wind
and music of joy whirling in the alleys

Tell her of the God of rainbows
and young inventors growing old

The courage
of Woman Life Freedom

But Dad,
don't tell her about the swinging noose searching for a neck
and what happens tomorrow at dawn

Please don't tell Mom

First published in *The Other Side of Hope*.

This poem was written in response to a young Iranian protester's phone call to his father from prison. "Dad, they have reached a verdict. Mine is execution by hanging. Don't tell Mom," whispered twenty-two-year-old Mohammad Mehdi Karami into the phone after the judge reached a verdict in a sham trial. A few weeks later he was executed.

Bänoo Zan

Urgent Report

IN THE NAME OF ALLAH

Urgent report to
the people of Iran
The Islamic Republic Officials
Chief Judiciary, Ministry of Intelligence, and
The Commander-in-Chief

I hereby inform you that
MY SON HOSSEIN IS UNDER TORTURE

I have just received A PHONE CALL
FROM AN UNKNOWN NUMBER
that they are taking Hossein
to the torture chamber in Evin Prison
to extract forced confessions from him

HOSSEIN IS VOMITING BLOOD
He is in very critical condition

NO ONE IN IRAN IS PAYING ATTENTION
Who is responsible?

Chief Judiciary,
I sent letters to you

IS TORTURE LEGAL IN THE ISLAMIC REPUBLIC?
Is torture legal in the constitution?
Is confession under torture acceptable to the courts?

THEY ARE KILLING HOSSEIN AS WE SPEAK
HOSSEIN IS UNDER TORTURE

Chief Judiciary, Your Honour,
You allow torture under your command
You cannot preside over the Department of Justice
Your officials are killing my son

THE GATE TO HUMAN RIGHTS IS CLOSED IN IRAN

In the Islamic Republic of Iran
the officials are not answerable
They are appointed to kill

GOVERNMENT OFFICIALS IN IRAN,
IS THIS SOCIAL JUSTICE?
IS THIS RELIGION?

Hossein is now under torture
by the intelligence

I HOPE YOU COME TO BELIEVE IN GOD
NONE OF YOU BELIEVE IN GOD
If you did, you wouldn't do this

I ask
all humans
all the world

I ask
all the countries
that respect human rights

I ask the United Nations,
The International Court of Justice in The Hague

and everyone in a position of influence—

to STOP THEM FROM KILLING MY SON

Hossein is under torture

If anything happens to Hossein
YOU ARE ALL RESPONSIBLE

ALL OF YOU—

First published in *Dissident Voice: A Radical Newsletter in the Struggle for Peace and Social Justice.*

This poem is based on a video posted to the Instagram account of Ahmad Ronaghi, the elderly father of the Iranian blogger and political dissident Hossein Ronaghi, on October 14, 2022.

WITNESS

Mary Gomez Fonseca

To Mahsa: From a Painter in Solidarity

I know what it is like to move openly in my mind
My thoughts effortless, smooth
My hand tracing an outline inside the page
of a body, tender flesh and bone
and blood that cuts across
doctrine and spits out metal and fire with each gesture

Drawing is an extension of writing.

I view the letters in newsprint,
with pictures of when she stood in curiosity and defiance
and declared herself to be
You. And only you.

Until she lost. And then won. And then lost again.
Her hair flowing like the end of a paintbrush
My hand steady to its vision
Swirling and caressing the danger

Your life, her death.
Our stories, unsaid and unseen
But what glory
can my images serve
to those who spell morality with fabric,
A twisted canvas wound as tight as gauze
over the skin of a Mother
oozing the sin of her unborn daughters

The cause of her, of you, of us.

Ehab Lotayef

Jin – Jiyan – Azadî

for Mahsa Amini

You walked into the sunrise
Now you are free
No prison cell can hold you
No knife can make you bleed
They say your name in pride
and chant: "A-za-dî"

They march for you in sorrow
chanting for the girls
who will be born tomorrow
Jin – Jiyan – Azadî

They choose to live their lives
To raise their heads up high
to laugh, to sing, to dance
to spread their wings and fly
Jin – Jiyan – Azadî

The world is yours, so speak
of freedom not of fear
Your scarf is yours to wear or tear
and march, defy and dare
and as you march you chant out loud,
so near and far will hear:

Women will be free!

The chant, Jin – Jiyan – Azadî in Kurdish translates to Woman, Life, Freedom.

Donna Langevin

Birdshot

The *Globe and Mail* lands
on my doorstep with a thump.
On the front page a young woman
with long, uncovered hair
wearing an eyepatch.

In photos on page 8, other protestors
blinded by guns loaded with birdshot
show off "badges of honour"
after the Islamic Revolutionary Guard
exploded their retinas
and they wept tears of blood.

Sparrows perch on my balcony railing.
I break peanuts into pieces.
The size of birdshot.
Watching them feed and fight, I'm awed
by that brave Kurdish woman who flew
in the face of the guard
and later posted to the world:
You aimed at my eyes, but my heart is still beating.

The name of the woman pictured on the front page of the *Globe and Mail*, January 12, 2024, is Mersedeh Shahinkar.

The quotation was posted on Instagram by another woman blinded by Iranian government forces, Elaheh Tavakolian.

Ayda Niknami

the pomegranate

it is the eighth day of the protests.
I have been crying all day from pain
and grief and hope and the weight of history.
we tried to go out dancing but there were
too many white people in the club.
now we are in your home (the one you share with her),
it is the first time we are really here alone:
purple lighting, flora, the Virgin
Mary hung high on the wall

there is a pomegranate on the windowsill.
it's been sitting there a while,
maybe even since you moved in—
but it's the fruit of knowledge,
you can't just let it rot
so I cut it open in your kitchen
while you lounge, your black Siamese
cats prowling around you

I cut off the crown
slice the fruit in half
pick each seed out with unsteady hands the
juice the blood of my homeland the juice
trickling down Saeid's chin as he laughed the
juice staining my mother's fingers as she
picked each seed out with unsteady hands

I come back from the kitchen
tiny white bowl filled with tiny pale reds
you put two in your mouth, wince
at the tartness, the bite
and I smile—it's an American
pomegranate, after all

I tell you about the pomegranates in Iran
scarlet, garnet, ruby, blood,
dark and sweet and sticky like the sin
they tried to bleed out of us

you are sleeping now
I am thinking of sin
I am thinking of Forough Farrokhzad's
poems in my mother's mouth

thinking of all the ways in
which 'woman' reads 'wrong'
and in how many languages?

as many as a pomegranate has seeds

Hollay Ghadery

I'm not supposed to be talking about this

it's not that big of a deal things are different when you're here you'd see everything is fine people are living their lives no blood in the streets no executions at dawn your cousin goes to school sees friends as she pleases doesn't live in fear the problem is the West is Western media making something out of nothing every country has its problems everyone loves a villain everyone talks of truth as if there's only one your country is young and youth thinks it knows everything knows best not to post this online you don't understand your cousin is well sends her love don't worry for us don't say you don't believe me come and see for yourself

Summer Brenner

Beautiful Stranger

He appears on a screen visible from faraway and looks directly at me and speaks

He looks and speaks in a soft voice, soft as a wave rolling onshore in soft Farsi words he speaks

His thick caterpillar brows and somber eyes perch like black doves over his beautiful nose

His soft words whisper like a leaf in the wind, echo like a child's voice trapped in a well

He says, *If you see this*
He says, *It means*
He says, *I've disappeared*

Elana Wolff
We felt like wearing orange sports caps

cycling up the mountainside,
                        riding in our bright
green cotton shirts.
We visioned being carried—
                                    light as autumn seed pods,
wheeling our legs like whirled batons,
                                    flinging our caps
behind us—   to the wind.
You on the rackety handlebars; I on the rickety seat.

We passed the place that burned to earth;
thousands gathered, ranting, chanting. Fervently,

we kept on cycling, you and I—
two women, pledged to azadi / to freedom.
                                        Up the mountain, resolute—
riding on our rightfulness, our colours,
                                                    & momentum.

azadi: freedom in Persian and Kurdish

Tanis MacDonald

Trace of Life

Mahsa Jina Amini's hair rises
in a sky-blue pouf and two goldfish swim
through it. She watches us all

pass. We are spoiling for a fight
on days when super-heated cowardice
scorches us. Her neck stretches

in a calm column from brick, to balance
her cloud-sprigged dairy-whipped turquoise
beehive as dream aquarium:

it's not over, resistance sings,
joy is not a crime. The day after the on-campus
stabbing, the university updates us

on security policy, and one woman
interrupts to say *where's the no-killing-women policy?*
They pause. The day breathes in with

the sound of Mahsa hashtagged.
Then they continue, advising all the assembled women
to teach in a room with two exits, to run.

The image described is a public mural, "The Trace of Life Left Behind" by the Olka Art Collective: Parisa Partovi, Ismaeil Rezaei, Leila Partovi, and Tania Sedighi.

Afsar Marefat
translated by Ari Honarvar

Even the pavement weeps

The old demons
have declared war on beauty and joy
They're bloodthirsty for jasmine and rose buds
Their enemy: love, music, and laughter

O beloved girl, where are you looking for love?
Every drunken lover is cut down in their prime
See, even the pavement weeps

O demons in power,
rancid poison is all you have to offer
Drink your own medicine
This century is no longer yours
This isn't the place for old executioners
It's time for you to choke on your own pollution

O beloved girl, you're bright as Venus,
Even in the blackest night
your blood lighting the way

Dawn is near
Believe me, my darling

Parastu Kamangir (Chang Shih Yen)
A Ghazal: Don't Forget Me

I'm gone from this world, but don't forget me.
I'm Mahsa Amini. Don't forget me.
I wanted to feel the sun warm my hair.
I've been martyred for that. Don't forget me.
My crime was letting the wind blow my hair.
I paid with my life, so don't forget me.
Live and love for me, now that I cannot.
Continue my fight, and don't forget me.
For all my sisters whose lives were cut short,
because we were murdered. Don't forget me.
Remember my name: Hadis Najafi,
Armita Geravand. Don't forget me.
Remember Sarina Esmailzadeh,
Forever sweet sixteen. Don't forget me.
Nasrin Ghaderi, Atefeh Naami,
Nika Shakarami. Don't forget me.
Forever fifteen, Asra Panahi,
Who will not swim again. Don't forget me.
How dare you kill old Minoo Majidi?
You'd kill your mother too? Don't forget me.
Remember the hundreds who were silenced.
Come out and shout loud: LIFE! Don't forget me.
I have lost my life, but gained my freedom
at the ultimate price. Don't forget me.
Look to the sky and see, like PARASTU,
I'm now free like a bird. Don't forget me.

The ghazal is a traditional form of Persian poetry. It was common for the poet to include their name or pseudonym in the last couplet. Here, Parastu is the poet's pen name. Parastu means the bird "swallow" in Persian.

Mansour Noorbakhsh

Make It a Rhyme

to all martyrs of "Woman, Life, Freedom"

If you come to see me, never come indifferently. Come like a fire needed for one lost in darkness. The light of an indelible intensity. Determined. I am a woman. I am not lost. My worry is that my footsteps may not have been heard. I'm afraid of twilight. How have they twisted virtue? Fading in darkness. They understand nothing when they look into our eyes. They exploit the twilight to shoot at our eyes. Without warning. My worry is that you may not have heard my footsteps. I am a woman. What words are they afraid of? My hair is an adverb of kindness. Bring me a light breeze and feet that walk freely. Freedom. A poem knows how to plant it like a seedling. Make it a verse of life. Plant a light. They exploit the twilight. They have stolen my life, and the eyes of many others. But not the freedom of walking in the light breeze of life. Make it a rhyme.

FUTURES

Sheida Mohamadi
translated by Mojdeh Bahar

My Feverish Bed Will Hallucinate Your Body

I am afraid I won't see you this fall
and the leaves piled at the door of your cottage
That this key won't turn through these spider webs
That something crow-shaped will fly out of the house.

I am afraid if I touch you
you'll wrinkle in the clouds
Your eyes will evaporate
My feverish bed will hallucinate your body
I'll turn to kiss you
You'll turn into dust in wind's memory.

I am afraid if I call you
people will know your beautiful name
They'll cut the trees' tongues
My tears will turn me into a starling
pitch black.

I am afraid if you come to my wedding
I won't be able to contain myself
and I'll burst out of the mirror
You'll bring me a wedding gift of thirty birds and forty parrots
and I'll no longer be in the hall of mirrors of Shiraz
That I'll be a lost dome
That you'll leave with the morning breeze
That a hoopoe will take you to Simorgh's fortress
unless you find me in traces of sunlight and moonlight,
in the reflection of Sheba's crystals.

I am afraid this *Shahnameh* will remain unfinished
That the dragon will come to your bedside
That your wings will catch fire and
that Simorgh will not recognize your scent in the mirror
I am afraid I'll be Tahmineh and not see you anymore
That nobody will recognize Sohrab's clasp
That they'll execute my sons in Tehran
That these boxwood branches will turn into double-headed arrows
That my entire being will long to see you
That Rostam will remain in the field of arrows and Bizhan in the pit.
I am afraid this fall you will escape to the darkness of my memory
That you'll find a three-year-old girl
gently hanging off of moonlit fences
That her mother will burn under the sun
That there'll be no one to wash her clothes in the moon's basin
I am afraid you'll escape to tomorrows
That my sister will unite with night and moonlight
and that they will find her baby in my uterus
That they'll explore my hair, strand by strand
in an inn in Masuleh
That they'll wrap a black shawl around me
That they'll stone me in the legend of Baba Leila.

I am afraid I'll appear in your dreams
like photos of thirty-year-olds
That you'll forget that I have become the widow of the wind
That you'll undress me and discover my breasts, two full moons shining
on the hot wilderness of Tassajara
That you won't see my body as an everlasting dream
my arms as light clouds
that creep toward darkness.

I am afraid I won't see you this fall
And the dream of a faraway land will tingle in the nails and fingers that
dig graves
That I'll pass by parallel lines
That hands will sing as they pass through customs
That they'll smell the scent of your wild heart among the clothes
That they'll find your kisses in my suitcase
That they'll compel me to confess
that you are the one who showed me the crows' refuge one fall day
And from that day on my body will smell of Golnar soap.

line 4: Crows are complicated symbols in Persian literature. They are portrayed as witty, yet can be outwitted; they are known to steal items such as food, bars of soap and shiny objects; and their song is supposed to be the herald of good news.

When telling stories to young children, the adult storyteller marks the conclusion by saying: "Our story has come to an end, yet the crow has not reached its nest." Here, the poem starts with the crow leaving its nest.

line 23: Reference to Attar's *Manteq-O-Teyr* or *The Conference of the Birds*, where the hoopoe is elected to lead the other birds to Simorgh.

Simorgh is a mythical bird; its name means "thirty birds."

line 25: This could reference the jewels that Suleiman offered Sheba. It could also serve as a reference to the floor of Suleiman's palace that was made of glass; Sheba mistook the glass for water.

line 26: *The Shahnameh* or *Book of Kings*, an epic poem written in the tenth and eleventh century by Abolqasem Ferdowsi.

line 30: This is a reference to the *Shahnameh*. In the Story of Sohrab, Tahmineh is Rostam's wife and Sohrab's mother. Sohrab went to war and was killed.

line 31: When Sohrab was leaving to go to war, his mother gave him a clasp that Rostam had gifted to her. Rostam had asked that should they have a son together, Tahmineh should give the clasp to him so he would know who his father is. During the fight, Rostam kills Sohrab and finds the clasp on his arm.

line 35: Rostam, realizing that he has mortally wounded his son, stays with his son's body in the field.

Another reference to the *Shahnameh* and the Story of Bizhan and Manizheh. Bizhan falls in love with the daughter of King Afrasyab, Manizheh. The king instructs his men to throw him into a dark pit weighed down by heavy chains.

line 47: *The Legend of Baba Leila* by Sheida Mohamadi is a novel that reflects the sociopolitical situation of its time. The novel depicts, among other things, the stoning of women in Iran.

line 64: Golnar soap was one of the most widely available bar soaps in the 1970s and 80s in Iran.

Fereshteh Molavi
Zhina

Zhina, the red poppy of Saqqez, blooms very strangely.
Scratch on throat, blisters on skin, pain in bone.
Bleeding.
The wounded body of woman takes refuge in the grave.
From the blood and the soil,
the field thrives with red stains of grief.

Zhina, the red poppy of Saqqez, wilts very quietly.
Yet the sea writhes in agony.
The Desert rants with rage.
Untamed girls cut their hair and let the wind take it away.

Zhina, the red poppy of Saqqez, follows her path persistently.
From the cold borders of rocky Kurdestan,
to Mount Sabalan and Sistan Desert,
to Khorasan region and Khuzestan plain.

Zhina wilts.
Zhina follows her path.
Zhina flies very lightly
towards freedom.
Her hair free in the air.
Zhina, the red poppy of Saqqez, blooms very strangely.

Rahil Najafabadi

When the World Moved On Without Me

I sat by my new bedding—it smelled like factory abuse
that I was funding. Floral and satin throw pillows
framing my insomnia. I take another bite of my painted
apple and it tastes like oil. I try to sleep but I'm reminded
I'm away from the mountains, and the sea will bury me
before I'm fifty. I wake up and think I must visit her more,
but I panic and cover myself with too many quilts.
I suffocate a little and only let one of my nostrils emerge
above the heat. I think of all the photographs of beautiful
cafes I deleted from my phone because there was no more
space. Instead, I store thirst traps I've never uploaded,
more bridges that take me farther from home. I delete
those too, and I illegally download folk songs from before
I was born. Somehow it moves me so much I feel tired
enough to drift. The world moved on without me,
from a revolution I wasn't here to stop. How do I start
a new one, without bringing new curses to a woman's home?

Azita Sadri
Fire

On fire for freedom,
my brothers and sisters march the street.

My cousin thinks, "If my scarf slips—will they hurt me?"

Brave Iranians holding up their fists in protest,
cutting their hair,
making their hearts bleed.
They exchange no nervous glances; they have no regard for the police.
Instead, they stand in their pain as they repeat, "*Zan, zendegi, azadi!*"

Tears flow between women, men, folks whose ideologies would never meet.
They think, "If this is how we unite, will our country ever see peace?"

Amongst the cries, I exhale a sigh of relief knowing that my
madarbozorg will never feel the pain of this country.
My family watches in fear hypothesizing that if she was here, she too
would be compelled to scream.
The pain of our people turned into hypothetical scenarios—an
attempt to escape this reality.
As another city ignites its fires, the conversation gets louder. So loud
that the room feels hotter.
So hot that my *baba* shrieks, "It feels like Abadan's heat!"

Amidst the chaos, there is hope that hangs above Iranian streets.
There are sentiments that the regime is changing, the regime is
changing…
but I ask,
"If it changes, will it still live inside me?"

My body washes in my country's warmth,
like the touch of a forbidden lover as I imagine my country being reborn.
I am weak to this thought, filled with childish hopes and dreams.
But as I smile, I realize that this warmth has turned into tears touching the sides of my cheek.
My tears roll, touching my hair. Suddenly, I am angry.
This hair that flows so free is a crime that they can't bear to see.
Hair. So soft yet so powerful,
something I wish to always be a part of me.

I start to wonder whose weapon really is this weaponized woman's hair.
Whether its thickness can be braided into ropes that we climb higher than they can see.
Whether each strand can turn into the strings of a harp, forming a choir that sings,
"*Zan, zendegi, azadi!*"

I cry in my hopeless despair thinking,
"Maybe it is too dangerous for us to be free."

madarbozorg: grandmother, in Persian
baba: father, in Persian

Kate Marshall Flaherty

Seven Shades of Rage

Anger: an intense emotion in response to perceived injustice;
from annoyance to fury

i)
first blush—pink spark of heat in the belly—
pastel before the purpling bruise

ii)
burgundy—afterglow like wine sting
spreading up the throat, salt sting—
awaiting release—

iii)
pomegranate—bitter seed and sharp pit
inside fruit's taut skin, bursting

iv)
ruby—gem's gleaming facets, so hard
it cuts through glass

v)
crimson—blood-pulse, throb in temple,
blue in vein, gush russet when cut:
sanguine

vi)
fire engine red—alarm! sirens! danger!
fire!

vii)
red-black—molten lava—fire in belly
spews forth   spit!   fury!
in a rage-spray of scorching rock-melt …

… that must move,
    must change …

must cool, eventually,
    to create new
        softer shapes …

Bänoo Zan

She Said, He Said

for Roya Heshmati

January 3, 2024
This morning, they contacted me from
the Sharia court to carry out the sentence.
I reported to the Public Prosecutor's Office
7th Division, Tehran, Iran.

The guard said:
Put your hijab on.

I said:
– I am here to be whipped
for not wearing a hijab!

The public executioner was summoned.
He said:
Put your hijab on
and come with me.

– I won't!

You won't? I'll lash you so you know where you are!
We'll also open a new case file on your dossier.
You will be served 74 more lashes!

I didn't put it on.

The man repeated the command:
Didn't I tell you to put it on?

I didn't put it on.

A woman in chador
pulled a scarf over my head.
          I removed it.

Back and forth …

They handcuffed me from the back,
pulled the scarf over my head.

We went down to the basement with
the judge, the public executioner, and the chadori woman.

The woman sighed: I know! I know!
The turbaned judge laughed in my face.
He reminded me of the old rag-and-bone man
in Sadegh Hedayat's *Blind Owl*.
          I turned my face away.

They opened an iron door
to a small room with cement walls
with a bed in the corner
with iron handcuffs and shackles.

By the bedside, there was an iron instrument
that looked like a painter's easel.

The judge asked:
How are you feeling, ma'am?
          I didn't respond.
I'm talking to you, ma'am!
          I didn't respond.

The public executioner said:
Remove your jacket.

I hanged my jacket and headscarf
from the torture easel.

He said:
Put your scarf on.

– I won't!
I said,
– Put your Quran under your arm,
as you should,
and lash me!

The woman came up:
Please don't be stubborn.
She pulled the scarf over my head.

The judge said:
Don't lash too sharply!

The man began.

He whipped me on my shoulders, shoulder blades, buttocks, thighs,
calves,
again and again …

I wasn't counting—was singing—
under my breath:

– In the name of woman
In the name of life
The cloak of slavery was rent
Our dark night will turn into dawn
and whips will break with the axe

It was finished.
We left.
I didn't let them think it hurt.

We went up to the office of
the public-executioner-judge.

I removed my hijab.
The woman said: Please put it on,
and pulled it over my head.

The judge said:
If you want to live differently
you can live abroad.

    I said:
    – This country belongs to all.

He said:
Yes. We're not happy either, but it's the law.

    I said:
    – Let the law do what it can.
    We'll continue our resistance.

We left the room.

And I removed my hijab.

First published in *Right Now: Human Rights in Australia.*

This story, which originally appeared on Roya Heshmati's social media, went viral among Iranians on the Internet.

the public executioner: The official responsible for carrying out sentences issued for violations of Hudood Ordinances, prescribed punishments for certain offences under the Islamic law.

Afterword

Against the Tyranny of Home: A Call for (Self-)Critique

"When the mirror reveals your image in truth,
break yourself. Don't break the mirror."*

—Nizami Ganjavi (1141–1209)

On September 16, 2022, Mahsa Jina Amini was murdered in custody of the so-called morality police in the Islamic Republic of Iran. Soon after, nationwide protests broke out across Iran in what came to be known as the Woman Life Freedom movement. On September 30, I sent the proposal for this anthology to Guernica Editions, and on October 5, we received the publisher's acceptance. The idea was to publish an international poetry anthology open to submissions from around the world regardless of the contributors' identity. This is a self-critical volume as well as a volume of solidarity.

The self-critique comes mainly from Iranians and people from the Middle East. But we cannot begin to criticize ourselves if we break the mirror that reflects ourselves back to ourselves. The outsider perspective situates us in the world. For our situation to change, we need to change. But we won't change if we don't admit that we have a hand in what we have brought upon our heads. There is no denying the fact that larger political forces have shaped the Middle East and Iran, but the "honour" is not all theirs.

It is easy to rant against outsiders, to blame them for our misery, to absolve ourselves of any responsibility.

It is easy to forget that the hell we escaped from was a hell, and that was why we left it behind. It is easy to forget that our own people

---

*آینه چون نقش تو بنمود راست
خود شکن، آیینه شکستن خطاست

were responsible for making our homeland so uninhabitable we had to leave.

It is easy to censor the critic, the truth-teller, the whistleblower, for fear that we may be found complicit in crimes committed in our name.

And, all crimes are committed in our name, especially the ones committed by our people—those whose blood is the same colour as ours; those who worship or renounce the same god(s); those who come from the same country, city, town, village, region, tribe, family, ethnicity, and race; those who speak the same language, listen to the same music, dance the same dances; those who share our politics, religion, gender, sexuality, and lifestyle.

In short, it is easy to write nostalgically about the idyllic fictional homelands. It is easy to self-stereotype, self-Orientalize, self-Occidentalize, self-pity.

And that is why there is a lot of nostalgic writing out there that portrays the refugees' or migrants' homelands as utopias. But that kind of writing has not initiated any meaningful change back home, as it has not told the whole truth. Writers and publishers are both complicit in this betrayal.

As an immigrant, I am fed up with expectations that want me to be an apologist or propagandist for my religion, culture, or country. I left my country because of homegrown corruption, violence, dictatorship, totalitarianism, cultural philistinism, misogyny, classism, xenophobia, racism, homophobia, and other forms of discrimination. These problems have existed in my dear homeland for centuries, if not millennia. They existed when we were an empire, when we were pagans, when we were Zoroastrians, when we were colonized by Islam, when we were invaded by the Eastern and Western powers, as well as when we declared independence. They are our particular brand, very Iranian, very Muslim, and very ex-Muslim—Iranian style. I cannot, in all honesty, accuse foreign powers of causing our problems. I did not leave Iran because of them. I left Iran because of Iranians. And this is the story of many refugees and migrants. We leave because of our cultures, religions, politics, and people.

It is impossible to separate culture from politics. Culture is reflected in politics. The dominant culture in Iran gives permission to one group of Iranians to censor other Iranians; attack them on the streets; arrest, jail, torture, and rape them; sentence them to death; and kill them under torture. This conformist culture gives permission to one group of Iranians to deprive other Iranians of their freedoms. It does not tolerate individuality and idiosyncrasy, in family or society, in private or in public. The political institutions in Iran have had similarities with other totalitarian regimes, but they have always been unmistakably Iranian.

Iranians, like other minorities in the West, come from a region that exports immigrants and refugees. It is time we asked ourselves difficult questions—not because we hate our land, but because we love it. Is it all the colonizers' fault? What have we been doing to ourselves before, during, and after contact with the West? Have we treated each other any better than outsiders, invaders, and colonizers have treated us? Our communities won't improve if we do not ask these questions openly in the public square. Silence has prevailed far too long. It has claimed far too many lives.

Dictators in our lands are happy that, in the West, we immigrants silence outsider as well as insider critics. They are happy when we write only about the greatness of our religion or culture. They are happy that publishers in the West print glowing stories about our part of the world. These blood-thirsty, corrupt dictators are grateful to the publishing industry in the West when it turns a blind eye to their crimes.

As writers and artists in exile, we may expect that our counterparts in the West—publishers, writers, activists—stand by us. Too often, we are disappointed. They are happy to believe whoever varnishes the truth about our part of the world because it gives them an excuse to disengage from our struggles against tyranny. They can then dismiss the cries of help coming from our civil society, dissident activists, and journalists. In this, we have ourselves to blame, as our own words have given our potential allies permission for indifference.

Enough of hypocrisy in life and in literature!

It is time to hold the enemy at home accountable.

Reader: Whoever you are and wherever you come from, the enemy is your enemy—and the home is your home. Because all people are your own people.

Challenge yourself and your own—humans all around the world—because in the absence of challenge, we regress—as we have done.

The job of a writer is to critique traditions, institutions, cultures, religions, customs, or nations. Epic and panegyric are passé. Our job is to write exposés.

If you are from country X, have lived under religion X, or are from race or ethnicity X, criticize X. If you are from minority Y in the larger community X, criticize Y. If you belong to opposition group O that seeks to subvert government Z, criticize O. In short, write about your own people's crimes against humanity; your own people's assaults against outsiders; your own people's suppression of others' freedoms and rights; your own people's corruption and violence; your own people's racism, xenophobia, sexism, and homophobia; your own people's imposition of superstition and religion on others; your own people's stupidity and ignorance and cruelty; your own people's crimes against your own people and others. Your own people's flaws. Spare no god or man of god, no politician or politics, no army or general, no relative or neighbour.

And, if you are an editor, a publisher, or a literary critic or judge; if you have a platform; and if out of ignorance, indifference, and cowardice you betray the truth, you are a henchman of dictators—unworthy of literature. Your platform is a truncheon that smashes protestors' skulls. Your pen is a bullet that blinds. Your awards are at the service of torture and intimidation and censorship. Your silence is a knife in the hand of an assassin.

This volume rants against the tyranny of home—against the hold it is allowed to have over us just because it is home—against all the injustice imposed on us in the name of religion, tradition, nation, and culture, whether sacred or secular—by our own people. Make no mistake, international community! This home is your own home. There is no one else to clean it up, wash the blood, break the chains, and tell stories of struggle and defeat.

All people are our own people with the right AND the responsibility to speak against injustice. As the anthology editors, we believe that women's rights are human rights, and that the erosion of women's rights anywhere is the erosion of women's rights everywhere. We accepted poems from around the world and reviewed the submissions without knowing the writers' identities. We encouraged the poets to explain words and concepts in footnotes to bring the poems closer to readers around the world. In the spirit of Woman Life Freedom, we treated no one as an insider or an outsider in the selection and editing of these poems. We are proud of what we have achieved.

When the mirror reveals your image in truth,
break yourself. Don't break the truth.

Bänoo Zan

Contributors

Ali Abdollahi, born in 1968 in Birjand, southern Khorasan, studied German in Tehran and lives in Berlin. A writer, literary critic, and translator, he has published eight volumes of poetry and over ninety translations, and has edited several poetry anthologies.

Alireza Adine was born in 1974 and is a current board member of the Iranian Writers' Association (founded in 1968). In about three decades, he has published five poetry books.

Ali Asadollahi, an Iranian poet and translator, is the author of six Persian poetry books. His poems and translations have appeared in *Bellingham Review, Denver Quarterly, Epoch, Hayden's Ferry Review, Los Angeles Review*, and others.

Mojdeh Bahar is an attorney, mediator, and translator. Her translations include *Milkvetch and Violets* (Mage, 2021 and 2024), *In the Mirror: Poems and Collages* (Gordyeh Publishers, 2023), and *Song of the Ground Jay*, Expanded Edition (Gordyeh Publishers, 2023).

Rasha Barrage is an Iraqi-born writer based in London. As a former lawyer, she has a particular interest in social justice issues. Her previous publications include *Say No to Racism* and *The Stoic's Guide to Life*.

Davood Bayat, an Iran-based poet and visual artist, has published two Persian poetry collections. He has had several conceptual art exhibitions around the country in collaboration with renowned domestic galleries.

Yvonne Blomer is a past poet laureate of Victoria, BC and the 2022–2023 Arc poetry magazine poet-in-residence. Her sixth book of poetry is *Death of Persephone: A Murder*. She lives on the territories of the Lək̓ʷəŋən-speaking people.

Summer Brenner is the author of a dozen books of poetry, short stories, noir crime, and social justice novels for youth. Her work has appeared in numerous literary journals and anthologies. Her most recent publication is *DUST, A Memoir* (2024).

Nilou Doust is a 21-year-old student who immigrated to Canada from Iran a little over a decade ago. She is currently studying Creative Expression and Society and English Literature at Victoria College in the University of Toronto.

Leila Farjami is a poet and psychotherapist. In addition to authoring several books of Persian poetry, her work has been recognized by *Nimrod Journal, Diode, Silk Road Review,* and more. Her poem "Caspian Sea" was nominated for a Pushcart Prize.

Kate Marshall Flaherty recently published *Titch* (Piquant Press). She has published in *CV2, Vallum, Grain, Room, Trinity Review, The Literary Review of Canada.* She writes spontaneous "Poems Of the Extraordinary Moment" (P.O.E.M.s) for charity, and guides StillPoint Poetry Circles. https://katemarshallflaherty.ca

Mary Gomez Fonseca is a professional voice actor for children's animation and is currently training in physical theatre for young audiences. She holds a Master's degree in Visual and Performance Art History and has taught and published in these areas.

Katerina Vaughan Fretwell's eleventh book, *Holy in My Nature* (Silver Bow) and tenth, *Familiar and Forgiveness* (Ace of Swords), appeared in 2024. *Dancing on a Pin* (Inanna, 2019) was longlisted for the Lowther Prize in IFOA's Battle of the Bards.

Mahdi Ganjavi (poet, literary translator, scholar, and publisher) has been a leading member of Iran's underground literature scene since the late 2000s. Ganjavi has published five volumes of poetry. He currently teaches at the Faculty of Information, University of Toronto.

Hollay Ghadery is an Iranian-Canadian multi-genre writer living in Ontario. *Fuse*, her memoir of mixed-race identity and mental health (Guernica Editions), won a Canadian Bookclub Award. She is the Poet Laureate of Scugog Township. www.hollayghadery.com

Ari Honarvar is the founder of *Rumi with a View*, dedicated to building bridges between the arts, social justice, and well-being, the author of the critically acclaimed novel *A Girl Called Rumi*, and the creator of Rumi's Gift Oracle Deck.

Noor Jafari is a poetry MFA student at Boston University. Her poems have appeared in *the engine(idling.*

Parastu Kamangir is the Persian pseudonym of **Chang Shih Yen**, a writer from East Malaysia, currently living in New Zealand. She has an MA degree in Linguistics, and speaks English, Malay, Chinese, Spanish and Portuguese. She is also learning Farsi.

Razia Karimi, born in Jaghori in Afghanistan's Ghazni province in 1994, has a degree in law. In 2022 she had to flee her homeland. Razia lives in Berlin, where she participates in multilingual writing workshops of The Poetry Project.

Ala Khaki is an Iranian poet, author of four poetry collections, a former political prisoner in Iran, and a former president of the Poetry Society of New Hampshire. His poems have appeared in Iranian and American literary journals and anthologies.

Donna Langevin's latest poetry collections are *Timed Radiance* (Aeolus House, 2022) and *Brimming* (Piquant Press, 2019). She and Kate Rogers co-authored the chapbook *Homeless City* (Aeolus House, 2024). Her play *Summer of Saints* was produced by Act2 STUDIO in 2022.

Ehab Lotayef is a poet, writer, lyricist, and justice activist of Egyptian origin, who moved to Canada in 1989. His works include *To Love*

a Palestinian Woman (TSAR, 2010) and the play *Crossing Gibraltar* (CBC, 2006). More at lotayef.com.

Tanis MacDonald (she/they) is the author of six books and works as an editor and professor in Waterloo, Ontario, Canada. Her latest book, *Straggle: Adventures in Walking While Female*, was published by Wolsak and Wynn in 2022.

Afsar Marefat is an Iranian poet and children's author. Her poetry collections, *Clarity of Mirrors* and *Waiting for Dawn*, have been published in Iran.

Sheida Mohamadi, poet, writer, scholar, journalist. Poet in Residence at UC Irvine (2015) and University of Maryland (2010), advocating Persian culture and literature. Authored six books, including *Hug Me Against the Haze*, and *I Blink and You Are a Peacock*.

Fereshteh Molavi is an Iranian-Canadian novelist and essayist who has been living in Toronto since 1998. She has published many books in Persian and several books in English. Her latest novel, *Thirty Shadow Birds*, was published by Inanna in 2019.

Anindita Mukherjee is a poet, scholar, and translator. Her first chapbook, *Nothing and Variations*, was featured in the top ten Young Indian Voices. Currently she is a participant in the 2024 Horizons Writers Circle, supported by the Edmonton Arts Council.

Rahil Najafabadi is a writer and multi-disciplinary artist living in New York City. Her work includes elements of womanhood, evolution of human emotion in the modern age, and guilt. Rahil was born in Tehran.

Ayda Niknami (she/they) is a Qashqai-Irani queer femme currently residing in "Vancouver." She is the incoming poetry editor for *PRISM International*, completing an MFA in Creative Writing at UBC, and holds an MA in Philosophy from UC San Diego.

Mansour Noorbakhsh is a bilingual poet whose poems echo themes of freedom, human rights, and the environment. He features The Contemporary Canadian Poets at https://persianradio.net/. Mansour's publications include *In Search of Shared Wishes* and poems in several anthologies.

Giovanna Riccio has authored three books of poetry: *Vittorio, Strong Bread,* and *Plastic's Republic,* a finalist for the 2022 Bressani Prize. Her work has appeared in national and international journals and anthologies, and has been translated into six languages.

Theresa Rüger studied Comparative Literature, Portuguese-Brazilian Studies, and English Philology in Berlin and Essex. She organizes multilingual poetic dialogues between young people with refugee backgrounds, edits and translates contemporary prose and poetry.

Siavash Saadlou is a Pushcart Prize-nominated writer. His poetry appears in *Porter House Review, Scoundrel Time,* and *CIRQUE,* among other journals. He is the winner of the 2023 Constance Rooke Nonfiction Prize and the 55th Cole Swensen Prize for Translation.

Azita Sadri, a Toronto-born writer, embodies her name's essence—free and ablaze. Culturally nurtured in a Persian-Filipino household, she crafts tales of love and culture, igniting conversations and championing the privilege of being heard.

Dana Serea is a student at Princeton University with work published in *The Daily Princetonian, Lunch Ticket, The Louisville Review,* and elsewhere. She has won several writing prizes and currently serves as a managing editor of *The Nassau Literary Review.*

Laura Sheahen is an American poet who splits her time between Maryland and Tunisia. She has travelled widely in Asia, Africa, and the Middle East as a writer for international charities.

Dr. Nilofar Shidmehr, a bilingual writer, poet, and creative writing-informed research scholar, has authored seven books of fiction and poetry, and served as a writer-in-residence in Canada. She teaches at SFU and is a Visiting Scholar at UBC.

Cy Strom has edited in different genres and sometimes languages, and has had a role in developing professional editorial standards and educational materials. He holds graduate degrees in early modern European history and has published in academic and other areas.

Elana Wolff is an award-winning author of poetry, essays on poems, original translations from the Hebrew, and a cross-genre Kafka-quest work titled *Faithfully Seeking Franz* (Guernica Editions, 2023). Her collection, *Swoon*, received the 2020 Canadian Jewish Literary Award for Poetry.

Diana Woodcock has authored six poetry collections, most recently *Heaven Underfoot* (winner, 2022 Codhill Press Pauline Uchmanowicz Poetry Award), *Holy Sparks* (Paraclete Press Poetry Award finalist), and *Facing Aridity* (Prism Prize for Climate Literature finalist). She teaches at VCUarts Qatar.

Bänoo Zan is a poet, translator, essayist, and poetry curator, with over 300 published pieces and three books. She is the founder of *Shab-e She'r* (Poetry Night), Canada's most diverse and brave poetry open mic series (inception 2012).

Acknowledgements

Early in September 2022, I began my term as Writer-in-Residence at the University of Alberta in Edmonton. On September 16, Mahsa Amini was murdered in the custody of the so-called morality police in the Islamic Republic of Iran. This event marked the start of the Woman Life Freedom revolutionary movement. On September 30, after securing the agreement of Cy Strom to work as my co-editor, I approached Guernica Editions with a proposal for this anthology. And, on October 5, the acceptance came.

We thank Michael Mirolla, Connie Guzzo-McParland and Anna van Valkenburg of Guernica Editions for accepting our proposal and for agreeing to our plan to make this an international anthology.

I thank the Writer-in-Residence committee members at the University of Alberta's English and Film Studies Department for the opportunity to serve as Writer-in-Residence for the academic year 2022–2023. Those nine months were among the best I have had in Canada.

Thanks go to all the journalists who interviewed me about my poetry projects and the upheavals in Iran, to magazines that published our poems and essays about the movement and this project, as well as to literary and community organizers who offered featured reading and speaking opportunities to share information about the project and the movement.

The list of individuals and literary magazines and journals that spread the word about this anthology and shared the call for submissions and for our fundraiser is too long to include here. They all have our gratitude. So do all those who contributed to our fundraiser. You can find the full list of financial contributors, as well as poets who appeared at our in-person fundraiser and artists who donated works for auction, on this anthology's Facebook page: https://www.facebook.com/WLFPoetryAnthology

This book owes its existence to the extraordinary courage and resilience of the Iranian women, men, and children who have been taking part in the ongoing Woman Life Freedom movement—the world's first feminist revolution.

MIX
Paper
FSC® C100212

Printed by Imprimerie Gauvin
Gatineau, Québec